British Insects

Victoria Munson

WAYLAND

Wayland, an imprint of Hachette Children's Group
Part of Hodder & Stoughton
Carmelite House, 50 Victoria Embankment
London EC4Y 0DZ

MIX
Paper from responsible sources
FSC
www.fsc.org FSC® C104740

Designer: Elaine Wilkinson
Consultant: Dr Tristan Bantock, Entomologist,
www.britishbugs.org.uk

A cataloguing record for this title is available
at the British Library.
Dewey number: 595.7'0941-dc23
ISBN: 978 0 7502 9321 1
ebook: 978 0 7502 9320 4

Printed in China

Wayland, part of Hachette Children's Group and
published by Hodder and Stoughton Limited.
www.hachette.co.uk

Acknowledgements:
Alamy: 12 Premaphotos; 48 Michael Rose;
51 Genevieve Vallee; 52 Daniel Borzynski;
Shutterstock: 4b Peter Waters; 5t Ian Grainger;
5b, 22 Chris2766; 6bl Nikiteev_Konstantin;
6br Stanislaw Tokarski; 7t manfredxy; 7m
richsouthwales; 7b Pixel Memoirs; 8 Brian
Maudsley; 9 Kletr; 10, 13, 15 Henrik Larssen;
11 bepsy; 14 Hector Ruiz Villar; 16 Hannu
Rama; 17 alslutsky; 18, 31 Martin Fowler; 18
inset Sari ONeal; 19 artconcept; 20 MarkMirror;
21 Elena Elisseeva; 21 inset Mark Mirror; 23
AdamEdwards; 24 Mirvav; 25 Peter Reijners; 25
inset HHelene; 26, 27 MarkMirror; 28 Milena
Lachowicz; 29 Bildagentur Zoonar GmbH; 30
Florian Andronache; 32 BHJ; 33 Fabio Sacchi;
34 Kletr; 35 Tom linster; 36 Arto Hakola; 37
Francesco Ocello; 38 EMJAY SMITH; 39 Torsten
Dietrich; 40 Arto Hakola; 41 PUMPZA; 42 Gurgen
Bakhshetsyan; 43, 45 main Marek R. Swadzba;
44 iliuta goean; 45 inset Jozef Sowa; 46 Platslee;
47 Florian Andronache; 49 PHOTO FUN; 50 Sue
Robinson; 53 DeZet; 54 Milena_; 55 Bildagentur
Zoonar GmbH; 56 Igor Semenov; 57 voylodyon;
58m Fedor Selivanov; 58b adv; 59 Peter Bull

Contents

Be a nature detective!

To be a nature detective, you need to be observant. This means looking around you. Insects can be seen all through the year, but summer is a good time to search for them because they are most active then.

What is an insect?

All insects have three parts to their bodies: a head, a thorax (middle) and an abdomen (lower part). On their head, they have a pair of antennae, which they use for smelling and feeling. Most insects have a pair of eyes and all insects have three pairs of jointed legs. Most adult insects have wings.

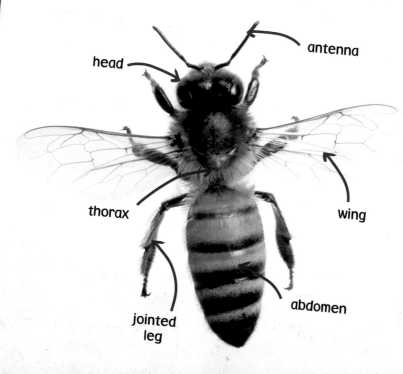

head

antenna

thorax

wing

jointed leg

abdomen

Some insects, such as butterflies, moths and bees, have a hollow tube called a proboscis through which they suck up food. Other insects, like Green Shield Bugs, have a pointed tube called a rostrum, which they use to pierce plants to suck up the sap. Beetles have strong jaws to bite and chew.

proboscis

Insect defence

Insects are eaten by many animals so they need different ways to protect themselves. Some insects sting, bite or produce poisons to shock their enemies, giving them time to get away. Other insects are brightly coloured to warn predators not to eat them. These insects usually have an unpleasant taste so predators remember not to eat them again. Camouflage can help to hide insects. Some insects look like the plants they eat, or are similar colours and markings to the leaves they feed on.

Red Soldier Beetles' bright colour warns away predators.

Look for insects on flowers or in between grasses.

How to identify insects

There are many different types of insects. Some of the most common are shown in this book, but you may see other, less common, types. It is a good idea to take a notebook out with you when nature spotting. Make a quick sketch and write down a description of the insect to help with identification.

Note down what colour it was, estimate its size and write where you saw the insect. Notice if it had wings and, if so, how many pairs. Did it have antennae? What was its leg shape? Some insects change shape and colour as they grow into adults. Males are often a different colour to females.

Saturday 12 June

Woodland walk   2.50pm

white spots

orange

black spots all over

an old dragonfly skin

Life cycles

Most insects are born from eggs. Eggs can be laid on the ground, on plants or in water. After birth, some insects change shape completely, others just get bigger. Insects such as earwigs and grasshoppers, look like smaller versions of the adults when they are born, but without wings. They are called nymphs at this stage. As these insects grow, their skin moults. A new skin grows under the old one. The old one splits and the insect wriggles out. Once they are adults, this doesn't happen again.

Cabbage White life cycle

Butterflies, moths, beetles, flies, ants and bees grow from eggs into larvae. They do not look like the adults. When the larva is big enough, it sheds its skin for the last time and becomes a pupa. Inside the pupa, the young insect changes into the adult insect.

eggs

larvae

butterfly

pupa

Seven-spot Ladybird

Scientific name: *Coccinella 7-punctata*
Size: up to 6 mm
Habitat: Gardens, parks and woodland

Ladybirds can beat their wings 85 times per second.

This small, round beetle has bright-red wing cases dotted with seven black spots. The bright colour warns predators that it tastes horrible. If a ladybird thinks it is about to be attacked, it will produce small blobs of yellow blood from its legs as a warning. In summer, female ladybirds lay clusters of eggs on leaves. The eggs hatch into small black larvae. The larvae have spiky grey-blue skin with yellow spots. The larvae turn into pupae, which become adult ladybirds in a couple of weeks.

22-spot Ladybird

Scientific name: *Psyllobora 22-punctata*
Size: 3–4 mm
Habitat: Grassland, woodland and gardens

These ladybirds are yellow with 11 black spots on each of their wing cases. They also have five spots behind the head (so they should really be called a 27-spot ladybird). The spots are more rounded than spots on the only other yellow and black ladybird, the 14-spot Ladybird. They feed on mildew on plants. In autumn, ladybirds group together in warm, dry places such as cracks in door frames or in between logs.

Red Soldier Beetle

Scientific name: *Rhagonycha fulva*
Size: up to 1 cm
Habitat: Gardens, parks and meadows

This long, narrow beetle has an orangey-red thorax and black-brown wing cases. Its bright colour is a warning to predators to stay away. Soldier Beetle larvae are flat, a dark brown-black and covered in hairs. The larvae live in the soil in winter and pupate in the spring. Red Soldier Beetles are also known as 'bloodsuckers'.

In summer, look for Soldier Beetles on Cow Parsley flower heads.

Stag Beetle

Scientific name: *Lucanus cervus*
Size: up to 50 mm
Habitat: Woodland

Stag Beetles are Britain's largest beetle, getting their name from the large jaws that look like a Stag Deer's antlers. They use these jaws to fight other male beetles. They have shiny, brown wing cases and a black thorax. Female Stag Beetles are smaller than males. Once a female has laid her eggs, she dies. Larvae are white and may spend up to six years feeding on wood before pupating in soil.

Green Tortoise Beetle

Scientific name: *Cassida viridis*
Size: 8–10 mm
Habitat: Gardens

Green Tortoise Beetles get their name because when they are disturbed, or feel threatened, they pull their antennae and feet in and pull their shell-like wing cases tightly down around them. Green Tortoise Beetles are lime green and a flattened, round shape. They are often found feeding on White Deadnettles.

Rhinoceros Beetle

Scientific name: *Sinodendron cylindricum*
Size: 1.5–1.8 cm
Habitat: Woodland, parks and hedgerows

Rhinoceros Beetles are large, cylinder-shaped beetles with a glossy blue-black back that is covered with small grooves. They are most recognised by the bump on their head that looks like a rhino's horn. Females have a much smaller bump than males. Rhinoceros Beetle larvae live in old trees and rotting wood. Look for Rhinoceros Beetles resting in the sun on dead tree trunks.

Great Diving Beetle

Scientific name: *Dytiscus marginalis*
Size: up to 4 cm
Habitat: Ponds

As the name suggests, these beetles lives in water, although at night you might also see them flying around. Great Diving Beetles are dark-brown to black with yellow legs and a yellow border around the head and thorax. Females have ridged wing cases while males have smooth. Males also have large sucker pads on their front legs. Both have strong jaws and are able to catch and eat large prey such as fish and newts.

Glow-worm

Scientific name: *Lampyris noctiluca*
Size: 1.5–2.5 cm
Habitat: Gardens, woods and hedgerows

Look for the glow from female Glow-worms in July and August.

These beetles get their name from the females, who can give out a greeny-orange light from their bottom in order to attract males. Females and larvae look similar; they are greyish-brown with yellowy-orange triangular markings at the side of each segment. Glow-worm larvae live under rocks and feed on slugs and snails. Male Glow-worms look like other types of beetles, with brown wing cases and a brown head.

Peacock

Scientific name: *Inachis io*
Wingspan: 6.5–7.5 cm
Habitat: Gardens, fields and orchards
Family: Nymphalids

Peacock caterpillars like to eat nettles.

This common garden butterfly has striking yellow and blue eyespots on the tip of each wing. These spots give the butterfly its name because they look like the markings on a peacock bird. In winter, Peacock butterflies hibernate in hollow trees and sheds.

Small Tortoiseshell

Scientific name: *Aglais urticae*
Wingspan: 4.5–6.2 cm
Habitat: Woodland, grassland, gardens, city centres
Family: Nymphalids

Small Tortoiseshell butterflies are bright orange with black and yellow bars on their forewings and black arches filled with blue edging on all four wings. Female Tortoiseshells can lay 80–100 eggs on the underside of nettle leaves.

Painted Lady

Scientific name: *Vanessa cardui*
Wingspan: 5.8–7.4 cm
Habitat: most habitats
Family: Nymphalids

Painted Ladies look very similar to Small Tortoiseshells, but Painted Ladies have more black patches and a large patch of black on the corner of each forewing that is dotted with white. The caterpillars have a black body with yellow stripes along it. Painted Lady butterflies come to Britain from Africa and the Mediterranean in March, and then all through the summer.

Look out for Red Admirals sucking juices from rotting fruit.

Red Admiral

Scientific name: *Vanessa atalanta*
Wingspan: 5.5–6 cm
Habitat: most habitats
Family: Nymphalids

These striking red and black butterflies are common visitors to gardens and are easily recognisable. They have bars of red on their fore and hindwings, with white spots on the tips of their forewings. The underside of their wings is a dark brown and black, which provides good camouflage when they rest on tree bark.

19

Comma

Scientific name: *Polygonia c-album*
Wing span: 5.5–6 cm
Habitat: Woodland
Family: Nymphalids

Commas were nearly extinct, but can now be found in southern England and are starting to spread north.

These butterflies are easily recognised by their curved and ragged wing edges. Commas are orange butterflies with black markings. Their undersides are brown with a white, comma-shaped mark. Commas like to rest head downwards on the bark of Birch or Ash trees, or on Bramble flowers and leaves.

Meadow Brown

Scientific name: *Maniola jurtina*
Wingspan: 4–6 cm
Habitat: Grassland, fields and meadows
Family: Browns

Meadow Browns are mainly brown with bright orange-brown patches on their forewings, in each of which is a black eyespot. These eyespots are used to scare away predators such as birds. Female Meadow Browns are slightly brighter-coloured than males and have a larger eyespot. Meadow Browns only live for about one month.

Speckled Wood butterflies like to perch in sunny spots.

Speckled Wood

Scientific name: *Pararge aegeria*
Wingspan: 4–5.5 cm
Habitat: Woodland, gardens and hedgerows
Family: Browns

Speckled Woods are mainly brown with creamy-yellow dots on the wings. They also have several eyespots; one on the tip of each forewing and three eyespots on each hindwing. Their undersides are a marbled light and dark brown. Females are larger than males and have slightly darker markings. Speckled Wood caterpillars are light yellowish-green with a dark-green stripe along the back and lines along the side.

Small White

Scientific name: *Pieris rapae*
Wingspan: 5 cm
Family: Whites and yellows
Habitat: Gardens, parks and farmland

One of the most common butterflies in Britain, the Small White is, as its name suggests, small and white. The females have two black spots and a black streak on the forewings. Males also have two black spots, but the second of these spots is much lighter. Small White caterpillars are a pest for farmers because they like to eat cabbages and Brussels sprouts.

Large White

Scientific name: *Pieris brassicae*
Wingspan: 6 cm
Habitat: Gardens, parks and farmland
Family: Whites and yellows

Large Whites are also known as 'Cabbage Whites'.

Large White butterflies look very similar to Small Whites, but Large Whites are, as the name gives away, much larger and their black markings are much darker. Females have two black spots while the males have no spots. Caterpillars are grey-green and mottled with black spots and yellow stripes. They stay as pupae through winter and adults emerge in spring. The caterpillars love to eat cabbages, so they are not popular with farmers.

Green-veined White

Scientific name: *Pieris napi*
Wingspan: 5 cm
Habitat: Woodland, meadows, hedgerows and riverbanks
Family: Whites and yellows

You can tell apart Green-veined Whites from Small Whites because, when their wings are closed, you can clearly see greenish-grey veins on the underwings. Green-veined Whites also prefer damp areas to the farmland and gardens where Small Whites are found. Green-veined Whites' forewings have a black tip. Males have a central black spot on the forewings and females have two spots.

Orange-tip

Scientific name: Anthocharis cardamines
Wingspan: 4.5–5 cm
Habitat: Riverbanks, hedgerows and meadows
Family: Whites and yellows

The best time to see Orange-tip butterflies is between mid-April and June.

Orange-tip butterflies get their name from the males that have striking orange tips on their white forewings. Female forewings are white, but with black tips and one black spot. Females look very similar to Small Whites, but Orange-tip males and females have mottled undersides.

Brimstone

Scientific name: *Gonepteryx rhamni*
Wingspan: 6 cm
Habitat: Grassland, damp woodland and hedgerows
Family: Whites and yellows

Brimstones have noticeably pointed, leaf-shaped wings. Females have pale green wings with an orange spot in the middle of each wing. Males have more yellowy-green underwings than females and yellow upperwings. Brimstones have a very long proboscis that helps them to feed on nectar deep inside flowers.

Poplar Hawk-moth

Scientific name: *Laothoe populi*
Wingspan: 1 cm
Habitat: Gardens, parks and woods
Family: Sphinx moths, Hawk moths
(Sphingidae)

Poplar Hawk-moths are grey or pinky
brown with hindwings that stick out in front of
the forewings when at rest. When threatened,
Poplar Hawk-moths flash the two bright-orange
patches on their hindwings. The patches are hidden
when the moth is resting. Caterpillars are bright green
with yellow stripes and a yellow horn-shape on their rear end.

Six-spot Burnet

Scientific name: *Zygaena filipendulae*
Wingspan: 2.5–4 cm
Habitat: Grasslands, sand dunes, meadows and marshes
Family: Burnets and Foresters (Zygaenidae)

Six-spot Burnet moths have black wings with six bright-red spots on each forewing. These are to warn away predators. Six-spot Burnet moths can be seen flying in the daytime. Females lay eggs on the leaves of a plant called 'Bird's-foot-trefoil'. Their caterpillars are pale yellow with black marks, and can be found resting at the bottom of these plants in winter before they become active again in spring.

Angle Shades

Scientific name: *Phlogophora meticulosa*
Wingspan: 5 cm
Habitat: Parks, gardens, woodland
and hedgerows
Family: Owlet (Noctuidae)

In the daytime, look for Angle Shades moths resting on fences.

This distinctive moth has pink and brown V-shaped markings on its wings. Its wings are crinkled at the edge, helping it to become camouflaged in leaves or on bark. Angle Shades caterpillars like to eat dock leaves and Stinging Nettles.

Elephant Hawk-moth

Scientific name: *Deilephila elpenor*
Wingspan: 6–7 cm
Habitat: Woodland, waste ground, streams and riverbanks
Family: Sphinx moths, Hawk moths (Sphingidae)

Elephant Hawk-moths get their name from the caterpillars, whose heads swell up in the shape of an elephant's head when they feel threatened. Elephant Hawk-moth caterpillars are brown-grey. Adults have pink and olive-green body parts with white legs and white antennae. You are most likely to see these moths in the evening, when they are visiting flowers to eat their nectar.

Common Wasp

Scientific name: *Vespula vulgaris*

Size: 2 cm

Habitat: Gardens, parks, grassland and woodland

There can be up to 2,000 wasps in one nest.

Common Wasps have a yellow and black head, a mainly black with yellow thorax and a yellow abdomen with black bands. They have yellow legs and black antennae. Large groups of Common Wasps live together in nests made from paper. The paper is made by the Wasps who chew small amounts of wood from trees and fences which is then mixed with saliva to form a papery pulp. The nests are usually made in holes in the ground.

Hornet

Scientific name: *Vespa crabro*
Size: up to 4 cm
Habitat: Parks and woodland

Hornets are wasps with a distinct 'waist'
between their thorax and abdomen. They have
two pairs of wings that are joined together by tiny
hooks, making it look like they have one pair of wings.
You can tell them apart from Common Wasps because
they have brown and yellow stripes, not black and yellow.
Hornets are also twice the size of Common Wasps.

Honey Bee

Scientific name: *Apis mellifera*
Size: 1.6 cm
Habitat: Gardens, parks, woodland

Honey Bees have slightly hairy, brown-black bodies with orangey-yellow bands and large black eyes. They will sting when they feel threatened, but once they have stung they die, unlike Common Wasps who can sting again and again. Honey Bees live together in large numbers in nests.

Early Bumblebee

Scientific name: *Bombus pratorum*
Size: around 1.6–1.8 cm
Habitat: Gardens, woodland and hedgerows

This common bumblebee gets its name from the queen bee who emerges from hibernation 'early' in spring. They are small bees with yellow bands on their black thorax and abdomen, and an orange tail. They group together in small colonies of around 100 workers, nesting underground or in old birds' nests.

Look for Early Bumblebees feeding on raspberries and blackberries.

White-tailed Bumblebee

Scientific name: *Bombus lucorum*
Size: up to 2.2 cm
Habitat: Gardens, farmland and woodland

White-tailed Bumblebees have a
distinctive white tail, and yellow bands on
the thorax and abdomen. They build large nests for
up to 400 workers underground in old mouse nests.

Common Carder Bee

Scientific name: *Bombus pascuorum*

Size: 1.3 cm

Habitat: Gardens, farmland, hedgerows and woodland

Common Carder Bees are easy to spot because they are the only bumblebee in Britain to have a completely reddish-brown thorax. They have darker brown bands on their abdomen. Their short coat looks scruffy. Males have longer antennae than females.

Red-tailed Bumblebee

Scientific name: *Bombus lapidarius*

Size: 2.3 cm

Habitat: Gardens, farmland, woodland and hedgerows

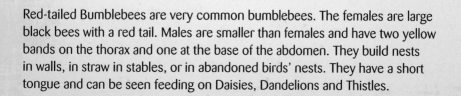

Red-tailed Bumblebees are very common bumblebees. The females are large black bees with a red tail. Males are smaller than females and have two yellow bands on the thorax and one at the base of the abdomen. They build nests in walls, in straw in stables, or in abandoned birds' nests. They have a short tongue and can be seen feeding on Daisies, Dandelions and Thistles.

Buff-tailed Bumblebee

Scientific name: *Bombus terrestris*

Size: 2 cm

Habitat: Gardens, farmland, woodland and hedgerows

Named after its 'buff-' or cream-coloured tail, this bee is very common across Britain. Worker bees have a white tail with a faint buff line separating the tail from the abdomen. They also have a dark yellowy-orange stripe near the head and another on the abdomen. Buff-tailed Bumblebees like to nest in the ground.

Black Garden Ant

Scientific name: *Lasius niger*
Size: up to 0.5 cm
Habitat: Gardens, parks, woodlands

Black Garden Ants live together
in huge colonies on the ground. Worker
Black Ants are wingless, brown-black females that
cannot breed. Each colony has one or two queen ants
that are much larger than worker ants. Male ants are smaller
than females and have wings.

Red Ant

Scientific name: *Myrmica rubra*
Size: 4 mm
Habitat: Gardens and fields

Red Ants have reddish-brown bodies. They live in colonies under stones, dead wood and in soil, and will attack any creature that disturbs their nest. There can be about 100 queens in one nest. Queen Red Ants can live for up to 15 years.

Common Field Grasshopper

Scientific name: *Chorthippus brunneus*
Size: 2 cm
Habitat: Grassy areas

Common Field Grasshoppers can be green, purple or black. They have narrow wings and can fly, but they usually use their long back legs to hop about instead. Females lay eggs in grass, protected by a foamy covering. Common Field Grasshoppers give out a short, brisk chirruping sound, which is made by rubbing their hind leg against their forewing.

Common Green Grasshopper

Scientific name: *Omocestus viridulus*

Size: 1.5–2 cm

Habitat: Grassy areas

Common Green Grasshoppers are the first of the grasshopper species to appear in spring. They are green with brownish sides. This grasshopper's song is long – lasting 20 seconds or more – and loud, making a noisy ticking sound.

Emperor Dragonfly

Scientific name: *Anax imperator*
Length: 7.8 cm length
Habitat: Ponds, lakes and rivers

Male Emperor Dragonflies have a bright blue-green body with a black stripe down the middle. Females are shorter with a greenish body that has a brown tip. Both have large eyes to help them detect prey. They catch their insect prey with their legs as they're flying, eating as they go unless it is a large insect in which case they stop to eat.

Banded Demoiselle Damselfly

Scientific name: *Calopteryx splendens*
Length: 4.8 cm
Habitat: Streams

female

male

Banded Demoiselle Damselflies are the largest damselfly in Britain. Males have a shiny metallic-blue body and their wings have a patch of blue. Females have a green body and green wings.

Large Red Damselfly

Scientific name: *Pyrrhosoma nymphula*
Length: 3.5 cm
Habitat: Ponds, lakes, rivers and canals

One of the earliest damselflies to appear
in spring, Large Red Damselflies are easy to
identify with their red and black body and black
legs. Adults don't get their full colour until they
are several days old. When resting, damselflies hold
their wings lengthways down their body, unlike dragonflies
who hold their wings outwards.

Common Earwig

Scientific name: *Forficula auricularia*
Size: 1.3–1.8 cm
Habitat: Gardens, parks and woodland

Earwigs got their name because of their ear-shaped wings.

Common Earwigs are easy to spot because they have prominent pincers at the rear end of their body. Male Earwigs have a pair of long curved pincers, while female pincers are smaller and straighter. Both have shiny brown bodies. Although they have wings, it is rare to see Common Earwigs flying. They are mostly nocturnal, coming out to feed at night.

Green Shield Bug

Scientific name: *Palomena prasina*
Size: 1.2–1.3 cm
Habitat: Gardens and woodland

These common garden bugs have a flattened 'shield'-shaped body. They are bright green with flecks of black. In winter, just before they hibernate, they become a darker colour. Females are larger than males. Both have sucking mouthparts to help them feed on plant sap.

Red-legged Shield Bug

Scientific name: *Pentatoma rufipes*
Size: 1.4 cm
Habitat: Woodland

Red-legged Shield Bugs are shiny brown with black and cream, or sometimes orange, markings around the edge of their wing cases. They have long antennae, which are about the same length as their body, and have square shoulders. In summer, adults lay eggs in the cracks of tree bark.

Pond Skater

Scientific name: *Gerris lacustris*
Size: 1.5 cm
Habitat: Ponds and lakes

Pond Skaters are small bugs with a brownish-black, narrow body. They have tiny hairs on their feet which repel water and allow them to 'skate' on the surface of ponds. They use their middle pair of legs to move themselves forwards with a rowing or jumping motion, and they use their rear pair of legs to steer left or right. The front pair of legs is used to catch and hold insects to eat.

Backswimmer

Scientific name: *Notonecta glauca*
Size: 1.8 cm
Habitat: Ponds, lakes and canals

Backswimmers are light brown with reddish eyes.
They swim upside-down, moving themselves through
water with their rear legs. While moving, they look like
the oars of a rowing boat. Their sides are covered with hairs
that trap air bubbles, making them look silvery in the water.
Backswimmers will eat insects, fish and tadpoles.

Froghopper

Scientific name: *Philaenus spumarius*

Size: 0.5 cm

Habitat: Woodland and fields

Adult Froghoppers are brilliant 'hoppers' and can leap 70 cm into the air, the equivalent to a human jumping over a block of flats! They can be a black or brown colour. Their wings fold like a tent over their body and their back legs trail behind them when they walk. Froghopper nymphs live in a protective frothy mass of bubbles on plants, especially Cuckoo Flowers, giving this mass of bubbles the name 'cuckoo spit'. The foam gives them moisture and protection from predators.

Lacewings

There are around 14 different species of green lacewing in Britain

Lacewing

Scientific name: *Chrysoperla carnea*
Size: up to 2 cm long
Habitat: Gardens, parks, woodland and meadows

Lacewings are very pale green with long antennae and golden eyes. In autumn, their body turns pinkish-brown. They have light-green, translucent, lacy wings that they fold like a tent around their abdomen. Lacewings are attracted by lights and therefore you are more likely to see them at night.

Mayfly

Scientific name: *Ephemera vulgata*
Size: 1–2 cm
Habitat: Rivers and lakes

Mayfly larvae spend 1–2 years
underwater feeding on algae and plants.
The adults hatch in summer and have very short
lives (from just one to a few days). Mayflies have wide,
clear, lace-like wings, short antennae and long thin tail bristles.
There are about 51 species of Mayfly in Britain and they look very
similar, with either two or three tail parts. One species of Mayfly does
emerge in May, giving it its name, but there are many species of Mayfly
that can be seen all year round.

Crane Fly

Scientific name: *Tipula paludosa*
Size: 2 cm
Habitat: Gardens, parks and grassy areas

Crane Flies have long, grey-brown bodies and long legs, which give them their nickname 'Daddy-Long-Legs'. Their two wings are thin and translucent. Crane Flies are attracted by lights, which is why they often fly into houses in the evening. They sometimes lose a leg trying to escape from a predator, but they can still survive without one or two legs.

Hoverfly

Scientific name: *Syrphus ribesii*
Size: 1 cm
Habitat: Gardens, woodland and hedgerows

Hoverflies are often confused with wasps and bees, but Hoverflies don't sting. They have a rounded, black body with yellow spots and bands. When resting, their wings still vibrate which makes a humming sound. Hoverflies are welcomed by farmers and gardeners because Hoverfly larvae feed on aphids found on berries. Aphids eat farmers' crops.

Marmalade Hoverfly

Scientific name: *Episyrphus balteatus*
Size: 0.9–1.2 mm
Habitat: Gardens, fields and meadows

Look for Marmalade Flies feeding on Cow Parsley.

This common hoverfly is mainly orange, with thick and thin, moustache-shaped, black bands across the body and large dark-red eyes. They can be seen in groups feeding on flowers like Tansy and Dandelion, and, at first glance, are often mistaken for wasps.

How to protect insects

Insects are important for several reasons. They are food for animals such as birds, bats, lizards and spiders. Many types of insects are needed to pollinate plants, so that we can grow crops. Insect habitats are under threat from road and house building, and from the use of weed killers in fields and gardens. Some species of insect in Britain are declining in numbers.

You can help!

Encourage insects into your garden by planting flowers and letting the grass grow long in one area. Long grass is important for egg-laying insects such as butterflies.

Tall flowers, such as Lavender and Foxglove, attract bees and dragonflies. Night-scented plants, such as Buddleia and Evening Primrose, are good for moths.

Ponds are home not only to insects, but to frogs, fish and newts, as well as providing water for birds. Why not ask your school to put a pond in the school grounds?

Make a ladybird home

Keep ladybirds safe and warm this winter by making a ladybird home.

1 Ask an adult to cut the end off a plastic drinks bottle.

2 Roll up the cardboard and push it tightly into the plastic bottle. Make sure the cardboard is all inside the bottle or it will get damp and the insects won't use it.

3 Tie some string around the bottle to hang it from a tree or shed. Make sure it won't swing around too much in the rain, or get wet inside.

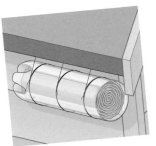

Other insects, as well as ladybirds, will probably use this home. They can rest through the winter and emerge again when the weather warms up in spring.

Look for ladybirds emerging from the bottle in spring.

Further information

Places to visit

National Trust

www.nationaltrust.org.uk/
visit/places/find-a-place-to-visit
Protecting a range of spaces
and places in England, Wales and
Northern Ireland, the National Trust
takes care of forests, woods, fens,
beaches, farmland, moorland and
nature reserves as well as historic
houses and gardens.
Find somewhere new to visit in your
local area or further afield.

The Wildlife Trusts

www.wildlifetrusts.org/reserves-wildlife/great-places-see/
dragonflies-and-damselflies

www.wildlifetrusts.org/woodlandbutterflies

www.wildlifetrusts.org/reserves-wildlife/great-places-see/
wildflower-meadows

The Wildlife Trusts website
recommends places across Britain
that are good for spotting all types
of insects, including dragonflies and
damselflies, as well as woodland
butterflies.

Useful websites

www.butterfly-conservation.org/679/a-z-of-butterflies.html

The Butterfly Conservation website has an excellent A-Z of butterflies and moths. This charity, with Sir David Attenborough as President, was set up to protect British butterflies and moths and their habitats. Every year, you can take part in their 'Big Butterfly Count' to help record butterfly species in the UK, so that steps can be taken to protect them if their numbers are found to be declining.

Go to www.bigbutterflycount.org in July and August to take part and to find out the results of last year's survey.

www.nhm.ac.uk/nature-online/life/insects-spiders

The Natural History Museum has an online identification guide for common insects and spiders.

www.nhm.ac.uk/nature-online/life/insects-spiders/ identification-guides-and-keys/bumblebees/index.html

Tips on how to identify bumblebees.

www.bumblebeeconservation.org/ get-involved/bumble-kids/

Find out all about Britain's bumblebees and learn how you can identify them and protect them.

Useful books

Extraordinary Bugs by Leon Gray (Wayland, 2012)

Usborne Spotter's Guide: Bugs and Insects by Anthony Wootton (Usborne, 2006)

Zoom in on Incredible Insects by Richard Spilsbury (Wayland, 2015)

How many different insects can you spot in your local area?

Glossary

abdomen the back part of an insect, joined to the thorax

antennae an insect's feelers, its sense organ for smell and touch

aphids very small insects

camouflage colours on an animal's body that blend with the background, making it difficult to spot

caterpillar the larva of a butterfly or moth

colony a group of insects that live together

extinct no longer existing

eyespot a spot that looks like an eye

forewing the front, or forward, wing of an insect

hibernate to spend the winter sleeping or resting

hindwing the back, or backward, wing of an insect

larvae the young of insects that hatch from their egg

mottled marked with coloured spots or areas

moults when an insect sheds its skin

nectar the sugary liquid produced by some flowers

nocturnal to be active at night

nymph the larva of an insect such as a dragonfly or damselfly

predator an animal that hunts and eats other animals

prey an animal that is hunted and eaten by another animal

proboscis the long, thin mouthpart of an insect

pupa (*plural: pupae*) the third stage in the life cycle of some insects

pupate to turn into a pupa

sap the liquid in plants

segment a part of an insect's abdomen

species one of the groups into which trees, plants and other living things are divided

thorax the middle part of the body of an insect – the legs and wings are attached to the thorax

translucent partly see-through

wingspan the distance from the tip of one wing to the tip of the other

Index